ROBERTO CLEMENTE
THE GREAT ONE

by James T. Olsen

Illustrated by Harold Henriksen

Text copyright © 1974 by Educreative Systems, Inc. Illustrations copyright © 1974 by Creative Education. International copyrights reserved in all countries. No part of this book may be reproduced in any form without written permission from the publisher. Printed in the United States.

Library of Congress Number: 73-13645   ISBN: 0-87191-279-1

Published by Creative Education, Mankato, Minnesota 56001
Prepared for the Publisher by Educreative Systems, Inc.
Distributed by Childrens Press, 1224 West Van Buren Street, Chicago, Illinois 60607

Library of Congress Cataloging in Publication Data
Educreative Systems, Inc.
   Roberto Clemente: the great one.
   (Its The Superstars)
   SUMMARY: Emphasizes the career and the kind deeds of a Puerto Rican baseball star.
   1. Clemente, Roberto, 1934-1972—Juvenile literature.
[1. Clemente, Roberto, 1934-1972. 2. Baseball Biography] I. Henriksen, Harold, illus. II. Title.
GV865.C45E38 1973 796.357'092'4[B] [92] 73-13645
ISBN 0-87191-279-1

Mr. and Mrs. Roberto Clemente walked into the furniture store. They had wanted to buy some furniture for their apartment for a long time. Roberto was a well known baseball star. He was also a hero to the Puerto Rican people. But at this particular furniture store, no one knew the Clementes. They had not even heard of them.

The salesman met the Clementes at the door of the store and asked: "What do you want?"

"We would like to see the showroom and see some furniture," Roberto answered. "We saw your ad in the newspaper and we saw some things we really liked. First . . ."

"Wait just a moment," the salesman cut in. "We have only one floor of furniture and we will have somebody take you there to see it."

The Clementes waited a little while. Finally, another salesman came and took them to the last floor of the building. "Here is some furniture for you to look at," the new salesman said.

"But I would also like to see the furniture in your showroom downstairs. That is what we saw advertised in the paper and that is what we are interested in buying."

The salesman turned to the Clementes. "Well, you don't have enough money to buy that. That is very expensive furniture."

Roberto looked at the salesman. "First of all, how do you know that I don't have enough money?" he asked. "And secondly, what right do you have to make up my mind for me?"

"But that furniture costs a lot of money," the salesman went on.

"I have the right to see it. I have the right to it as a human being, as a person who comes to buy from you."

Finally, the salesman took the Clementes downstairs to the front showroom. Now Roberto looked at the salesman. He reached into his pocket and pulled out his wallet. He took five thousand dollars from his wallet and waved it in front of the salesman's nose. "Do you think this much money can buy this furniture?"

"I'm sorry, Sir, I . . ."

Another salesman walked by. He stopped suddenly in his tracks. He came over to Roberto. "Roberto Clemente!" he said. "It is really an honor to have you in our store."

The first salesman looked at the Clementes. "I'm sorry, Sir," he said. "We thought you were like any other Puerto Rican."

Roberto looked at both of the salesmen. "Look, your business is to sell to anybody. I don't care if I'm Puerto Rican or if I'm Jewish, or whatever you want to call me."

With those words, Roberto put his money back into his wallet. He took his wife's arm and stormed out of the store. "Maybe next time, you'll know just a little better!" he yelled back over his shoulder.

Roberto Clemente was not only a great baseball player. He was also a man who had strong feelings about other people. Even when he had "made it" he never forgot what it was like to be poor or to be a Puerto Rican in a white man's world.

It was so early in the morning that the sky was still black. The streets of the Comandante section of Rio Piedras were almost empty. Rio Piedras was a town about ten miles southeast of San Juan, Puerto Rico. Moving slowly from house to house was a small boy. He was carrying heavy cans of milk. It was his job to deliver them. He had to get up very early, and finish his work before he went to school. For all his hard work, this little boy only earned 30 cents a month. It took him three years to save up enough money to buy a second hand bicycle. That little boy was Roberto Clemente.

Roberto was born on August 18, 1934. He was the youngest child in a large and happy family. The family worked together, and helped each other. But Roberto's life was not all work.

Along with his job and school, Roberto also played baseball. His older brother, Justino, was also a baseball player. Young Roberto kept an album of his brother's baseball feats. Roberto wrote about his own feeling for baseball. "I love the game so much that even though our playing field was muddy and we had many trees on it, I used to play many hours every day."

That early ball field was an important place for Roberto. On that field, he learned the skills that were to make him such a great baseball player when he got older. The fences were about 150 feet away from home plate and Roberto says that he used to hit "many homers every day." There was one game he especially remembered. That game started at eleven o'clock in the morning and finished at about 6:30 that night. In that game, Roberto hit ten home runs.

Roberto's family was very happy even though they were very poor. Roberto was always close to his parents. In one of his interviews, Roberto said, "I was so happy because my brothers and my father and my mother, we used to get together at night, and we used to sit down and make jokes, and we used to eat whatever we had to eat."

"And this was something that was wonderful to me. I grew up with people who really had to struggle to eat. During the war when food was hard to get, my

parents fed their children first and they took what was left. They always thought of us."

Roberto's mother was the first person to see how interested in baseball he really was. His mother, Luisa Walker de Clemente said, "Roberto was born to play baseball. I can remember when he was five years old. He used to buy rubber balls every time he had a chance. He played in his room, throwing the ball against the wall and trying to catch it. There were times when he was so much in love with baseball that he didn't even care for food."

When Roberto went to high school he played more baseball. He made the all-star baseball team three years in a row, as a shortstop. Baseball, however, was not the only high school sport that Roberto played. He was also a track star. Roberto was the school's "Most Valuable Player." He threw the javelin 195 feet. He was a six foot high jumper. He went forty five feet in the triple jump. He was an outstanding young athlete.

Little did Roberto Clemente know that the park in which he played high school baseball would one day be renamed for him: The Roberto Clemente Park.

When Roberto was eighteen and still in high school, he showed up at a park where the Santurce Crabbers, a Puerto Rican baseball team, were playing. He went on the field with them as a shortstop. The man who owned the team, Pete Zorilla, watched Roberto. Zorilla looked at Clemente and said very simply, "You can play for me right now." And so Roberto Clemente joined the team for $500.00 and a new baseball glove.

Roberto played very well with that team. The manager of the team, Jim Clarkson, remembers Roberto very well: "The big thing about Roberto was that he played very hard and went all out in every game. He did that when he was just a kid, and he did that all the way up through his last season. He was always on the offense. He pushed himself. I saw that from the first. Maybe that was the thing about him as a ballplayer that people will remember most."

After he had been playing for the Crabbers for a while, Roberto was again noticed by another baseball scout. This scout, Al Campanis, recalls that Roberto "was the greatest natural athlete I have ever seen."

Campanis goes on to describe the tryout for the Brooklyn Dodgers. "The first thing we do at a tryout is to ask the kids to throw from the outfield. This one throws a bullet from the center, on the fly, I couldn't believe my eyes."

"Uno mas," I shout. "And he does it again. I waved my hand. That's enough. Then we have them run 60 yards. The first time I clock him in 6.4 seconds. I couldn't believe it. That's in full uniform."

"Uno mas," I shout again. "And he did it again. In 6.4 seconds. I sent the other players home. The only one I asked to hit was this fellow, who told me his name was Roberto Clemente. He hit for twenty, twenty-five minutes. I'm behind the cage, and I'm saying to myself, we gotta sign this guy if he can just hold the bat in his hands."

"He starts hitting line drives all over the place. I notice the way he's standing in the box, and I figure there is no way he can reach the outside of the plate, so I tell the pitcher to pitch him outside, and the kid swings with both feet off the ground and hits line drives to the right and sharp ground balls up the middle."

The following spring, the Dodgers offered Roberto a contract for ten thousand dollars. Roberto signed and was on his way as a big league baseball player.

Shortly afterwards, Roberto was traded to the Pittsburgh Pirates for $4,000. In the beginning, Roberto had trouble getting along with his manager. When Roberto would get mad because something didn't go his way, he would break the plastic batting helmets and even the baseball bats. One day, Roberto's manager felt that he had had enough of Roberto's show of temper. He said to Roberto: "I don't mind you tearing up your clothes if you want to. But if you want to break club property you're going to have to pay for it."

Roberto also remembered those days. As he himself put it, "Once, I break 22 helmets. Haney, he tells me it will cost $10.00 for each one. That's $220.00, and I do not make so much money. I stop breaking helmets."

Roberto went on to say that this lesson helped him to learn how to control his temper. He also said that in the end it helped to make him a better ball player. Roberto needed to learn how to control his feelings because some players tried to put him down for being a Puerto Rican. In one game, for example, Roberto made an excellent catch. The catch robbed the batter of an extra base hit. As he trotted to the dugout at the end of the inning, the batter passed by him and called him a name—a name that wasn't nice at all.

Roberto did not understand the batter very well. He was still learning English and didn't know the meaning of what the batter had said. So Roberto simply said, "Thank you." One of Roberto's teammates heard what the other batter had said and told Clemente, "Do you know what he called you?" The teammate told Roberto what the other batter meant. Roberto thanked his teammate. When he went back out on the field, Roberto passed the batter and returned the remark to him three times. The other batter said nothing.

Then came the World Series. The team that was playing against the Pirates was the New York Yankees. Everyone thought that the Yankees would win easily. The Pirates won the first game 6-4. Roberto had one hit and drove in one run. New York then took the second game and then the third. The Pirates took games four and five with the Yankees tieing the series by taking the sixth.

The final seventh game! In the bottom of the eighth inning the Yankees were ahead. The Pirates came back at them with five runs to move ahead 9-7. Back and forth the score went. The crowd was going wild. In the ninth inning, the Pirates finally moved ahead and won with a score of 10-9.

Roberto Clemente played in that series. And he played very well! He got a hit in every game. He was the fourteenth player in baseball history to hit safely in every game of a World's Series. There were seven games in all and Roberto felt that he had proven himself finally as one of the great baseball players of all time. He felt that he should get the Most Valuable Player of the Year Award.

Roberto did not receive the award that year. He did receive it later, though. And more than that, he was also honored by his team, the Pittsburgh Pirates, on July 24, 1970. On that night, called "Roberto Clemente Night" 43,290 people came out to honor Roberto. Many people in the crowd were Puerto Ricans who had come to see and honor their hero. That night meant a great deal to Roberto: "In a moment like this you can see a lot of years in a few minutes. You can see everything firm and you can see everything clear."

"I don't know if I cried, I am not ashamed to cry. I would say a man never cries from shame or from disappointment, but if you know the history of our island, the way we were brought up, you ought to remember we're a people who show our feelings."

"I don't have the word to say how I feel when I step on that field, and know that so many are behind me, and know that I represent my island and Latin America."

In the off season, when Roberto wasn't playing baseball, he had many other interests. One of his dreams was to build a "Sports City" for Puerto Rican youngsters. Roberto wanted to have a special place for youngsters to learn sports. These young people would have the best sport's coaches around to show them how to play any sport that they really wanted to be good at. Roberto said, "Lots of kids don't play in sports because they don't like one certain sport. But if you have all sports in one place where they can play, I bet you that kids will like at least one of them and keep going with that."

Roberto wanted very much to help young people in any way that he knew how. He knew how hard it had been for him. He felt that he could make it easier for other youngsters who would be coming after him. "Any time you are able to do something for somebody who comes behind you and you don't do it, you are wasting your time on this earth."

It was natural for Roberto to feel this way. As far as baseball was concerned, he was now called "The Great One." And there was no question that he was. Four times, he was Batting Champion of the National League! In 1966, he was voted the Most Valuable Player of the League. He was the winner of the Golden Glove for Fielding Proficiency twelve times, the Most Valuable Player of the Pittsburgh Pirates 1971 World Series Victory, and the eleventh man in the history of baseball to make 3,000 hits. That is quite a list of baseball awards! There was no question that Clemente was now at the height of his professional career. It is an interesting thing about Roberto that at such a moment he was thinking about people who were not as fortunate as he was.

Roberto was a true superstar. But he was also a very special man. The last act of his life proves this.

During the month of December in 1972, thousands of people had been killed in an earthquake. That earthquake had almost completely destroyed the capital city of Managua in Nicaragua. Most people had read about the earthquake in the newspapers or they had seen it on television. Roberto Clemente was one of the people who had read about it. He thought that these thousands of people needed help. They needed food, clothing, and medical care. While the Nicaraguan government was doing all it could do, Roberto felt

that others should help, too.

Roberto decided that he would help Puerto Rico help Nicaraguans. He thought that he could head up the aid sent by Puerto Ricans. But what could he really do? He was only one man. He could of course give money. But he felt that was too easy. So he started collecting food and clothing for the people of Managua. Some people said that Roberto was just trying to get some publicity for himself, see his name in the newspapers. Others said that he was just letting some of the aid groups use his name, but that he himself wasn't really doing anything.

Those people were very wrong. They did not understand how deep Roberto's feelings really went. As a matter of fact, on New Year's Eve, when most people were going to parties and having a good time, Roberto was at the San Juan airport. The reason he was there was that he was directing the loading of food and clothing onto an old D. C. 7 airplane. Roberto planned to stay on the plane until it got to Nicaragua. There, he would see to it that the people who needed these supplies really got them! Then he planned to return to Puerto Rico and spend New Year's Day with his own family.

But there was trouble at the airport. First of all, the pilot was late. Secondly, the plane wasn't working right. It seemed to be having mechanical problems. The take-off had been put off a number of times because of these problems. Roberto was eager to get started because he wanted to get back to his family. He knew that the sooner he got there, the sooner he would be with his family to celebrate the New Year. Roberto finally said while he was at the airport, "If there is one more delay, we'll leave this for tomorrow."

Roberto's wife, Vera, was also worried. She felt that the plane was very old. Too old! She felt that the plane was overloaded. She told Roberto that she didn't think he should leave on the plane. She didn't have good feelings about the trip. But Roberto felt that the problems would be solved and that they would get to Nicaragua without any new problems. He finally said to her, "Vera, just be sure to have roast pork for me and the kids when I get back. And tell Roberto Jr., Luis, and Enrique to be good while I'm gone."

And with those words, Roberto boarded the old plane with the food and clothing on it. Those were the last words he ever spoke to anyone. On New Year's Day, 1973, the search for the missing plane began. It turned out that the plane had crashed into the ocean. It was finally found 120 feet beneath the surface of the water by a diver. On January 14, 1973, Governor Rafael Hernandez Colon held the funeral service for Roberto Clemente in San Juan, Puerto Rico.

Along with the whole world, his fellow Puerto Ricans mourned the death of Roberto Clemente. Somehow, Roberto had died remembering the words of his father who had told him, "I want you to be a good man, I want you to work, and I want you to be a

serious person." Roberto had lived his life following
that advice and carrying it out in everything he did.
As people thought back over his life, they thought of
all the kind things that Roberto had done for them.

His history teacher in Puerto Rico, Mrs. Caceres,
remembered what he had done for her. Each year,
Roberto would visit her when he went home at the
end of the baseball season. She tells about the time he
came to visit her at school and they told him that she
was sick at home. Roberto went to her house and
learned from her how badly she really felt. After he
had listened for a while, Roberto took her up in his
arms. He lifted her right out of the bed and took her
to a doctor! He took her to the doctor every day like

that until she was able to walk again.

Mrs. Caceres finally asked Roberto how much the doctor had cost him. She wanted to pay him back the money he had spent on her. Roberto became very angry with her and told her that she was not to ask him about the doctor again. He said that when she asked him such a question, she hurt his feelings. He said that he was making plenty of money and that she did not have to worry about it at all. Roberto certainly wasn't worrying about it, either.

Every winter, Roberto would also stop by his old school to say hello to the students. He would spend about a day talking with them and telling them about professional baseball and things like that. Before he was killed, he had planned to spend a day with them right after New Year's. Of course, he was never able to make that meeting, but there had been so many in the past that the students remembered him. The students said that he had made a difference to them because he brought with him all kinds of new ideas. He encouraged them to do the kinds of things they wanted to do with their lives. He told them that they could be successful. That the most important thing was to remember the people who would be coming after them. They should work hard so that they will be able to help all of the other people not as fortunate as they were.

Those were the kinds of ideas that Roberto Clemente tried to give to people. He tried to do this not only through words and talks, but also through his own actions. In a way, it was very natural for him to have died the way that he did. He died trying to help people who were not as fortunate as he. He died trying to help his fellow men in the most basic way possible, through giving food and clothing to people whose homes had been wiped out in a single stroke.

This was the side of Roberto Clemente that the baseball fans never really saw. Because for all of his help to people, Roberto was a very private person who did not go to parties very often. He did not even go to the after-game parties that the Pirates had in their lockerroom after a victory. He just didn't feel that he had the time for that kind of thing. He felt that baseball was only one part of his life. His job there was to do the best he could, to give his all to the game. And he led his team. In later years, the team members of the Pittsburgh Pirates talked about Roberto as "our inspiration." That he certainly was! Not only to his teammates, either. Roberto Clemente was an inspiration to all men and women who value those who make it a little bit easier for the ones who come after them. And that is something that Roberto did. And like everything else he did, he did it well!

3 Indy
Wins

CREATIVE'S
SUPERSTARS

Mark Spitz	Billie Jean King
Jackie Robinson	Vince Lombardi
Johnny Bench	Roberto Clemente
Wilt Chamberlain	Jack Nicklaus
Joe Namath	Jerry West
A. J. Foyt	Bobby Hull
Arnold Palmer	Muhammad Ali
Bill Russell	O. J. Simpson
Tom Seaver	Hank Aaron